BACK UP! THIS DIARY BELONGS TO:

_____
INSERT NAME

Hey Girl!

Your teenage years are the most trying, fun, and confusing years all at one time. You're constantly changing friends, your sense of style, classes, tastes in music and activities, and even your feelings towards yourself! But the great news is, you'll make it through your teen years just fine, and the good news is, you're not alone.

My Crazy Teenage Life Diary is your personal sacred space to jot down your thoughts about yourself, school, friends, family, and your future. It's also a safe place for daily reflections and to monitor your feelings. This is your diary to unload everything from your happiest thoughts to what made you feel uncomfortable from day to day. You'll even have space to write whatever you want to, whenever you want to, and as much as you wish. When this diary becomes full, simply get another one, and save them all - because as each year passes by, you'll be able to take a look at your diaries and see how much progress you have made as you advance through your crazy teenage years!

Xo,

Kinyatta

I'M A TEEN.
I SPEND MOST OF MY TIME IN MY ROOM. I SPEND A LOT OF TIME ONLINE. I HAVE PRIVATE THINGS ON MY PHONE.
I GO TO BED LATE & I'M CRAZY ABOUT ONE PERSON.

~UNKNOWN

7-DAYS
OF SELF-LOVE QUOTES

SUNDAY
"You are capable of amazing things."

MONDAY
"You glow from the inside out."

TUESDAY
"Your smile, your walk, your talk and your style are your superpowers." ~Kinyatta E. Gray

WEDNESDAY
"Your value doesn't decrease based on someone's inability to see your worth." ~UNKNOWN

THURSDAY
"Be careful of how you speak to yourself since you are listening." ~Lisa Hayes

FRIDAY
"Why fit in when you were born to stand out?" ~Dr. Suess

SATURDAY
"Your future is created by what you do today, not tomorrow."
~ Robert Kiyosak

25 THINGS THAT MAKE ME SMILE

1. _____
2. _____
3. _____
4. _____
5. _____
6. _____
7. _____
8. _____
9. _____
10. _____
11. _____
12. _____
13. _____
14. _____
15. _____
16. _____
17. _____
18. _____
19. _____
20. _____
21. _____
22. _____
23. _____
24. _____
25. _____

DESCRIBE YOURSELF IN 30 WORDS.
WHO ARE YOU?

1. _____
2. _____
3. _____
4. _____
5. _____
6. _____
7. _____
8. _____
9. _____
10. _____
11. _____
12. _____
13. _____
14. _____
15. _____
16. _____
17. _____
18. _____
19. _____
20. _____
21. _____
22. _____
23. _____
24. _____
25. _____
26. _____
27. _____
28. _____
29. _____
30. _____

MY THOUGHTS ABOUT HIGH SCHOOL...

_____
_____
_____
_____
_____
_____
_____
_____
_____
_____
_____
_____
_____
_____
_____
_____
_____
_____
_____
_____
_____
_____
_____
_____
_____

MY THOUGHTS ABOUT HIGH SCHOOL....

MY THOUGHTS ABOUT HIGH SCHOOL...

MY THOUGHTS ABOUT COLLEGE...

MY THOUGHTS ABOUT COLLEGE...

MY THOUGHTS ABOUT COLLEGE...

_____
_____
_____
_____
_____
_____
_____
_____
_____
_____
_____
_____
_____
_____
_____
_____
_____
_____
_____
_____
_____
_____
_____

MY THOUGHTS ABOUT A FUTURE CAREER AND ENTREPRENEURSHIP...

MY THOUGHTS ABOUT A FUTURE CAREER AND ENTREPRENEURSHIP...

MY THOUGHTS ABOUT A FUTURE CAREER AND ENTREPRENEURSHIP...

MY THOUGHTS ABOUT MY SPECIAL TALENTS (SINGING, MAKEUP ARTISTRY, ATHLETICISM) ...

_____
_____
_____
_____
_____
_____
_____
_____
_____
_____
_____
_____
_____
_____
_____
_____
_____
_____
_____
_____
_____

MY THOUGHTS ABOUT MY SPECIAL TALENTS (SINGING, MAKEUP ARTISTRY, ATHLETICISM) ...

_____
_____
_____
_____
_____
_____
_____
_____
_____
_____
_____
_____
_____
_____
_____
_____
_____
_____
_____
_____
_____
_____

MY THOUGHTS ABOUT MY SPECIAL TALENTS (SINGING, MAKEUP ARTISTRY, ATHLETICISM) ...

_____
_____
_____
_____
_____
_____
_____
_____
_____
_____
_____
_____
_____
_____
_____
_____
_____
_____
_____
_____
_____

MY THOUGHTS ABOUT MY FAMILY...

_____
_____
_____
_____
_____
_____
_____
_____
_____
_____
_____
_____
_____
_____
_____
_____
_____
_____
_____
_____
_____
_____
_____

MY THOUGHTS ABOUT MY FAMILY...

MY THOUGHTS ABOUT MY FAMILY...

MY THOUGHTS ABOUT MY FRIENDS...

_____
_____
_____
_____
_____
_____
_____
_____
_____
_____
_____
_____
_____
_____
_____
_____
_____
_____
_____
_____
_____
_____
_____
_____

MY THOUGHTS ABOUT MY FRIENDS...

MY THOUGHTS ABOUT MY FRIENDS...

I'M FRUSTRATED BY...

_____
_____
_____
_____
_____
_____
_____
_____
_____
_____
_____
_____
_____
_____
_____
_____
_____
_____
_____
_____
_____
_____

I'M FRUSTRATED BY...

___

I'M FRUSTRATED BY...

MY Crazy TEENAGE LIFE SELF-REFLECTIONS

Date: /   /

When I need support, I can count on…	**Today I Feel:** ☐ Fabulous ☐ In love ☐ Kind of sad ☐ Frustrated ☐ Lonely ☐ Anger ☐ Tired
My favorite song today is…	
I felt inspired when…	

I felt happiest when…
When I'm bored I…
I felt uncomfortable/sad when…

School was…	My parents…
My friends were…	My siblings…

When I think of "someone special" I feel…
I am grateful for…
This was hard but I overcame it by:
This is what I will remember most about today:

MY Crazy TEENAGE LIFE SELF-REFLECTIONS

Date: /   /

When I need support, I can count on…	**Today I Feel:**
My favorite song today is…	☐ Fabulous ☐ In love ☐ Kind of sad ☐ Frustrated
I felt inspired when…	☐ Lonely ☐ Anger ☐ Tired

I felt happiest when…

When I'm bored I…

I felt uncomfortable/sad when…

School was…	My parents…
My friends were…	My siblings…

When I think of "someone special" I feel…

I am grateful for…

This was hard but I overcame it by:

This is what I will remember most about today:

MY Crazy TEENAGE LIFE SELF-REFLECTIONS

Date: /   /

When I need support, I can count on…	**Today I Feel:** ☐ Fabulous ☐ In love ☐ Kind of sad ☐ Frustrated ☐ Lonely ☐ Anger ☐ Tired
My favorite song today is…	
I felt inspired when…	

I felt happiest when…
When I'm bored I…
I felt uncomfortable/sad when…

School was…	My parents…
My friends were…	My siblings…

When I think of "someone special" I feel…
I am grateful for…
This was hard but I overcame it by:
This is what I will remember most about today:

MY Crazy TEENAGE LIFE SELF-REFLECTIONS

Date: /   /

When I need support, I can count on...	**Today I Feel:**
	☐ Fabulous
My favorite song today is...	☐ In love
	☐ Kind of sad
	☐ Frustrated
I felt inspired when...	☐ Lonely
	☐ Anger
	☐ Tired

I felt happiest when...

When I'm bored I...

I felt uncomfortable/sad when...

School was...	My parents...
My friends were...	My siblings...

When I think of "someone special" I feel...

I am grateful for...

This was hard but I overcame it by:

This is what I will remember most about today:

MY Crazy TEENAGE LIFE SELF-REFLECTIONS

Date: /   /

When I need support, I can count on…	**Today I Feel:** ☐ Fabulous ☐ In love ☐ Kind of sad ☐ Frustrated ☐ Lonely ☐ Anger ☐ Tired
My favorite song today is…	
I felt inspired when…	

I felt happiest when…
When I'm bored I…
I felt uncomfortable/sad when…

School was…	My parents…
My friends were…	My siblings…

When I think of "someone special" I feel…
I am grateful for…
This was hard but I overcame it by:
This is what I will remember most about today:

MY Crazy TEENAGE LIFE SELF-REFLECTIONS

Date: / /

When I need support, I can count on…	**Today I Feel:**
	☐ Fabulous
My favorite song today is…	☐ In love
	☐ Kind of sad
	☐ Frustrated
I felt inspired when…	☐ Lonely
	☐ Anger
	☐ Tired

I felt happiest when…

When I'm bored I…

I felt uncomfortable/sad when…

School was…	My parents…
My friends were…	My siblings…

When I think of "someone special" I feel…

I am grateful for…

This was hard but I overcame it by:

This is what I will remember most about today:

MY Crazy TEENAGE LIFE SELF-REFLECTIONS

Date: /   /

When I need support, I can count on…	**Today I Feel:**
My favorite song today is…	☐ Fabulous ☐ In love ☐ Kind of sad ☐ Frustrated
I felt inspired when…	☐ Lonely ☐ Anger ☐ Tired

I felt happiest when…
When I'm bored I…
I felt uncomfortable/sad when…

School was…	My parents…
My friends were…	My siblings…

When I think of "someone special" I feel…
I am grateful for…
This was hard but I overcame it by:
This is what I will remember most about today:

MY Crazy TEENAGE LIFE SELF-REFLECTIONS

Date: /   /

When I need support, I can count on...	**Today I Feel:** ☐ Fabulous ☐ In love ☐ Kind of sad ☐ Frustrated ☐ Lonely ☐ Anger ☐ Tired
My favorite song today is...	
I felt inspired when...	

I felt happiest when...

When I'm bored I...

I felt uncomfortable/sad when...

School was...	My parents...
My friends were...	My siblings...

When I think of "someone special" I feel...

I am grateful for...

This was hard but I overcame it by:

This is what I will remember most about today:

MY Crazy TEENAGE LIFE SELF-REFLECTIONS

Date: /   /

When I need support, I can count on…	**Today I Feel:**
	☐ Fabulous
My favorite song today is…	☐ In love
	☐ Kind of sad
	☐ Frustrated
I felt inspired when…	☐ Lonely
	☐ Anger
	☐ Tired

I felt happiest when…

When I'm bored I…

I felt uncomfortable/sad when…

School was…	My parents…
My friends were…	My siblings…

When I think of "someone special" I feel…

I am grateful for…

This was hard but I overcame it by:

This is what I will remember most about today:

MY Crazy TEENAGE LIFE SELF-REFLECTIONS

Date: /   /

When I need support, I can count on…	**Today I Feel:** ☐ Fabulous ☐ In love ☐ Kind of sad ☐ Frustrated ☐ Lonely ☐ Anger ☐ Tired
My favorite song today is…	
I felt inspired when…	

I felt happiest when…

When I'm bored I…

I felt uncomfortable/sad when…

School was…	My parents…
My friends were…	My siblings…

When I think of "someone special" I feel…
I am grateful for…
This was hard but I overcame it by:
This is what I will remember most about today:

MY Crazy TEENAGE LIFE SELF-REFLECTIONS

Date: /   /

When I need support, I can count on…	**Today I Feel:**
	☐ Fabulous
My favorite song today is…	☐ In love
	☐ Kind of sad
	☐ Frustrated
I felt inspired when…	☐ Lonely
	☐ Anger
	☐ Tired

I felt happiest when…

When I'm bored I…

I felt uncomfortable/sad when…

School was…	My parents…
My friends were…	My siblings…

When I think of "someone special" I feel…

I am grateful for…

This was hard but I overcame it by:

This is what I will remember most about today:

MY Crazy TEENAGE LIFE SELF-REFLECTIONS

Date: /   /

When I need support, I can count on...	**Today I Feel:** ☐ Fabulous ☐ In love ☐ Kind of sad ☐ Frustrated ☐ Lonely ☐ Anger ☐ Tired
My favorite song today is...	
I felt inspired when...	

I felt happiest when...
When I'm bored I...
I felt uncomfortable/sad when...

School was...	My parents...
My friends were...	My siblings...

When I think of "someone special" I feel...
I am grateful for...
This was hard but I overcame it by:
This is what I will remember most about today:

MY Crazy TEENAGE LIFE SELF-REFLECTIONS

Date: /   /

When I need support, I can count on...	**Today I Feel:** ☐ Fabulous ☐ In love ☐ Kind of sad ☐ Frustrated ☐ Lonely ☐ Anger ☐ Tired
My favorite song today is...	
I felt inspired when...	

I felt happiest when...
When I'm bored I...
I felt uncomfortable/sad when...

School was...	My parents...
My friends were...	My siblings...

When I think of "someone special" I feel...
I am grateful for...
This was hard but I overcame it by:
This is what I will remember most about today:

MY Crazy TEENAGE LIFE SELF-REFLECTIONS

Date: /   /

When I need support, I can count on...	**Today I Feel:** ☐ Fabulous ☐ In love ☐ Kind of sad ☐ Frustrated ☐ Lonely ☐ Anger ☐ Tired
My favorite song today is...	
I felt inspired when...	

I felt happiest when...
When I'm bored I...
I felt uncomfortable/sad when...

School was...	My parents...
My friends were...	My siblings...

When I think of "someone special" I feel...
I am grateful for...
This was hard but I overcame it by:
This is what I will remember most about today:

MY Crazy TEENAGE LIFE SELF-REFLECTIONS

Date: /   /

When I need support, I can count on…	**Today I Feel:**
My favorite song today is…	☐ Fabulous ☐ In love ☐ Kind of sad ☐ Frustrated
I felt inspired when…	☐ Lonely ☐ Anger ☐ Tired

I felt happiest when…

When I'm bored I…

I felt uncomfortable/sad when…

School was…	My parents…
My friends were…	My siblings…

When I think of "someone special" I feel…

I am grateful for…

This was hard but I overcame it by:

This is what I will remember most about today:

MY Crazy TEENAGE LIFE SELF-REFLECTIONS

Date: /   /

When I need support, I can count on…	**Today I Feel:** ☐ Fabulous ☐ In love ☐ Kind of sad ☐ Frustrated ☐ Lonely ☐ Anger ☐ Tired
My favorite song today is…	
I felt inspired when…	

I felt happiest when…
When I'm bored I…
I felt uncomfortable/sad when…

School was…	My parents…
My friends were…	My siblings…

When I think of "someone special" I feel…
I am grateful for…
This was hard but I overcame it by:
This is what I will remember most about today:

MY Crazy TEENAGE LIFE SELF-REFLECTIONS

Date: /   /

When I need support, I can count on…	**Today I Feel:**
	☐ Fabulous
My favorite song today is…	☐ In love
	☐ Kind of sad
	☐ Frustrated
I felt inspired when…	☐ Lonely
	☐ Anger
	☐ Tired

I felt happiest when…

When I'm bored I…

I felt uncomfortable/sad when…

School was…	My parents…
My friends were…	My siblings…

When I think of "someone special" I feel…

I am grateful for…

This was hard but I overcame it by:

This is what I will remember most about today:

MY Crazy TEENAGE LIFE SELF-REFLECTIONS

Date: /   /

When I need support, I can count on…	**Today I Feel:** ☐ Fabulous ☐ In love ☐ Kind of sad ☐ Frustrated ☐ Lonely ☐ Anger ☐ Tired
My favorite song today is…	
I felt inspired when…	

I felt happiest when…
When I'm bored I…
I felt uncomfortable/sad when…

School was…	My parents…
My friends were…	My siblings…

When I think of "someone special" I feel…
I am grateful for…
This was hard but I overcame it by:
This is what I will remember most about today:

MY Crazy TEENAGE LIFE SELF-REFLECTIONS

Date: /   /

When I need support, I can count on...	**Today I Feel:**
My favorite song today is...	☐ Fabulous
	☐ In love
I felt inspired when...	☐ Kind of sad
	☐ Frustrated
	☐ Lonely
	☐ Anger
	☐ Tired

I felt happiest when...

When I'm bored I...

I felt uncomfortable/sad when...

School was...	My parents...
My friends were...	My siblings...

When I think of "someone special" I feel...

I am grateful for...

This was hard but I overcame it by:

This is what I will remember most about today:

MY Crazy TEENAGE LIFE SELF-REFLECTIONS

Date: /   /

When I need support, I can count on…	**Today I Feel:** ☐ Fabulous ☐ In love ☐ Kind of sad ☐ Frustrated ☐ Lonely ☐ Anger ☐ Tired
My favorite song today is…	
I felt inspired when…	

I felt happiest when…

When I'm bored I…

I felt uncomfortable/sad when…

School was…	My parents…
My friends were…	My siblings…

When I think of "someone special" I feel…

I am grateful for…

This was hard but I overcame it by:

This is what I will remember most about today:

MY Crazy TEENAGE LIFE SELF-REFLECTIONS

Date: /   /

When I need support, I can count on...	**Today I Feel:**
	☐ Fabulous
My favorite song today is...	☐ In love
	☐ Kind of sad
	☐ Frustrated
I felt inspired when...	☐ Lonely
	☐ Anger
	☐ Tired

I felt happiest when...

When I'm bored I...

I felt uncomfortable/sad when...

School was...	My parents...
My friends were...	My siblings...

When I think of "someone special" I feel...

I am grateful for...

This was hard but I overcame it by:

This is what I will remember most about today:

MY Crazy TEENAGE LIFE SELF-REFLECTIONS

Date: /   /

When I need support, I can count on…	**Today I Feel:** ☐ Fabulous ☐ In love ☐ Kind of sad ☐ Frustrated ☐ Lonely ☐ Anger ☐ Tired
My favorite song today is…	
I felt inspired when…	

I felt happiest when…
When I'm bored I…
I felt uncomfortable/sad when…

School was…	My parents…
My friends were…	My siblings…

When I think of "someone special" I feel…
I am grateful for…
This was hard but I overcame it by:
This is what I will remember most about today:

MY Crazy TEENAGE LIFE SELF-REFLECTIONS

Date: /   /

When I need support, I can count on...	**Today I Feel:**
My favorite song today is...	☐ Fabulous
	☐ In love
	☐ Kind of sad
I felt inspired when...	☐ Frustrated
	☐ Lonely
	☐ Anger
	☐ Tired

I felt happiest when...

When I'm bored I...

I felt uncomfortable/sad when...

School was...	My parents...
My friends were...	My siblings...

When I think of "someone special" I feel...

I am grateful for...

This was hard but I overcame it by:

This is what I will remember most about today:

MY Crazy TEENAGE LIFE SELF-REFLECTIONS

Date: /   /

When I need support, I can count on…	**Today I Feel:** ☐ Fabulous ☐ In love ☐ Kind of sad ☐ Frustrated ☐ Lonely ☐ Anger ☐ Tired
My favorite song today is…	
I felt inspired when…	

I felt happiest when…
When I'm bored I…
I felt uncomfortable/sad when…

School was…	My parents…
My friends were…	My siblings…

When I think of "someone special" I feel…
I am grateful for…
This was hard but I overcame it by:
This is what I will remember most about today:

MY Crazy TEENAGE LIFE SELF-REFLECTIONS

Date: / /

When I need support, I can count on…	**Today I Feel:**
	☐ Fabulous
My favorite song today is…	☐ In love
	☐ Kind of sad
	☐ Frustrated
I felt inspired when…	☐ Lonely
	☐ Anger
	☐ Tired

I felt happiest when…

When I'm bored I…

I felt uncomfortable/sad when…

School was…	My parents…
My friends were…	My siblings…

When I think of "someone special" I feel…

I am grateful for…

This was hard but I overcame it by:

This is what I will remember most about today:

MY Crazy TEENAGE LIFE SELF-REFLECTIONS

Date: /   /

When I need support, I can count on…	**Today I Feel:** ☐ Fabulous ☐ In love ☐ Kind of sad ☐ Frustrated ☐ Lonely ☐ Anger ☐ Tired
My favorite song today is…	
I felt inspired when…	

I felt happiest when…
When I'm bored I…
I felt uncomfortable/sad when…

School was…	My parents…
My friends were…	My siblings…

When I think of "someone special" I feel…
I am grateful for…
This was hard but I overcame it by:
This is what I will remember most about today:

MY Crazy TEENAGE LIFE SELF-REFLECTIONS

Date: / /

When I need support, I can count on...	**Today I Feel:**
	☐ Fabulous
My favorite song today is...	☐ In love
	☐ Kind of sad
	☐ Frustrated
I felt inspired when...	☐ Lonely
	☐ Anger
	☐ Tired

I felt happiest when...

When I'm bored I...

I felt uncomfortable/sad when...

School was...	My parents...
My friends were...	My siblings...

When I think of "someone special" I feel...

I am grateful for...

This was hard but I overcame it by:

This is what I will remember most about today:

MY Crazy TEENAGE LIFE SELF-REFLECTIONS

Date: /   /

When I need support, I can count on…	**Today I Feel:** ☐ Fabulous ☐ In love ☐ Kind of sad ☐ Frustrated ☐ Lonely ☐ Anger ☐ Tired
My favorite song today is…	
I felt inspired when…	

I felt happiest when…

When I'm bored I…

I felt uncomfortable/sad when…

School was…	My parents…
My friends were…	My siblings…

When I think of "someone special" I feel…

I am grateful for…

This was hard but I overcame it by:

This is what I will remember most about today:

MY Crazy TEENAGE LIFE SELF-REFLECTIONS

Date: /   /

When I need support, I can count on…	**Today I Feel:**
My favorite song today is…	☐ Fabulous ☐ In love ☐ Kind of sad ☐ Frustrated
I felt inspired when…	☐ Lonely ☐ Anger ☐ Tired

I felt happiest when…

When I'm bored I…

I felt uncomfortable/sad when…

School was…	My parents…
My friends were…	My siblings…

When I think of "someone special" I feel…

I am grateful for…

This was hard but I overcame it by:

This is what I will remember most about today:

MY Crazy TEENAGE LIFE SELF-REFLECTIONS

Date: / /

When I need support, I can count on…	**Today I Feel:** ☐ Fabulous ☐ In love ☐ Kind of sad ☐ Frustrated ☐ Lonely ☐ Anger ☐ Tired
My favorite song today is…	
I felt inspired when…	

I felt happiest when…
When I'm bored I…
I felt uncomfortable/sad when…

School was…	My parents…
My friends were…	My siblings…

When I think of "someone special" I feel…
I am grateful for…
This was hard but I overcame it by:
This is what I will remember most about today:

MY Crazy TEENAGE LIFE SELF-REFLECTIONS

Date: /   /

When I need support, I can count on...	**Today I Feel:**
My favorite song today is...	☐ Fabulous
	☐ In love
	☐ Kind of sad
I felt inspired when...	☐ Frustrated
	☐ Lonely
	☐ Anger
	☐ Tired

I felt happiest when...

When I'm bored I...

I felt uncomfortable/sad when...

School was...	My parents...
My friends were...	My siblings...

When I think of "someone special" I feel...

I am grateful for...

This was hard but I overcame it by:

This is what I will remember most about today:

MY Crazy TEENAGE LIFE SELF-REFLECTIONS

Date: /   /

When I need support, I can count on…	**Today I Feel:**
	☐ Fabulous
My favorite song today is…	☐ In love
	☐ Kind of sad
	☐ Frustrated
I felt inspired when…	☐ Lonely
	☐ Anger
	☐ Tired

I felt happiest when…

When I'm bored I…

I felt uncomfortable/sad when…

School was…	My parents…
My friends were…	My siblings…

When I think of "someone special" I feel…
I am grateful for…
This was hard but I overcame it by:
This is what I will remember most about today:

MY Crazy TEENAGE LIFE SELF-REFLECTIONS

Date: /   /

When I need support, I can count on…	**Today I Feel:**
My favorite song today is…	☐ Fabulous
	☐ In love
I felt inspired when…	☐ Kind of sad
	☐ Frustrated
	☐ Lonely
	☐ Anger
	☐ Tired

I felt happiest when…
When I'm bored I…
I felt uncomfortable/sad when…

School was…	My parents…
My friends were…	My siblings…

When I think of "someone special" I feel…
I am grateful for…
This was hard but I overcame it by:
This is what I will remember most about today:

MY Crazy TEENAGE LIFE SELF-REFLECTIONS

Date: /   /

When I need support, I can count on…	**Today I Feel:** ☐ Fabulous ☐ In love ☐ Kind of sad ☐ Frustrated ☐ Lonely ☐ Anger ☐ Tired
My favorite song today is…	
I felt inspired when…	

I felt happiest when…
When I'm bored I…
I felt uncomfortable/sad when…

School was…	My parents…
My friends were…	My siblings…

When I think of "someone special" I feel…
I am grateful for…
This was hard but I overcame it by:
This is what I will remember most about today:

MY Crazy TEENAGE LIFE SELF-REFLECTIONS

Date: / /

When I need support, I can count on…	**Today I Feel:**
My favorite song today is…	☐ Fabulous ☐ In love ☐ Kind of sad ☐ Frustrated
I felt inspired when…	☐ Lonely ☐ Anger ☐ Tired

I felt happiest when…

When I'm bored I…

I felt uncomfortable/sad when…

School was…	My parents…
My friends were…	My siblings…

When I think of "someone special" I feel…

I am grateful for…

This was hard but I overcame it by:

This is what I will remember most about today:

MY Crazy TEENAGE LIFE SELF-REFLECTIONS

Date: /   /

When I need support, I can count on…	**Today I Feel:**
	☐ Fabulous
My favorite song today is…	☐ In love
	☐ Kind of sad
	☐ Frustrated
I felt inspired when…	☐ Lonely
	☐ Anger
	☐ Tired

I felt happiest when…

When I'm bored I…

I felt uncomfortable/sad when…

School was…	My parents…
My friends were…	My siblings…

When I think of "someone special" I feel…

I am grateful for…

This was hard but I overcame it by:

This is what I will remember most about today:

MY Crazy TEENAGE LIFE SELF-REFLECTIONS

Date: /   /

When I need support, I can count on…	**Today I Feel:**
	☐ Fabulous
My favorite song today is…	☐ In love
	☐ Kind of sad
	☐ Frustrated
I felt inspired when…	☐ Lonely
	☐ Anger
	☐ Tired

I felt happiest when…

When I'm bored I…

I felt uncomfortable/sad when…

School was…	My parents…
My friends were…	My siblings…

When I think of "someone special" I feel…

I am grateful for…

This was hard but I overcame it by:

This is what I will remember most about today:

MY Crazy TEENAGE LIFE SELF-REFLECTIONS

Date: /   /

When I need support, I can count on…	**Today I Feel:**
My favorite song today is…	☐ Fabulous
	☐ In love
	☐ Kind of sad
I felt inspired when…	☐ Frustrated
	☐ Lonely
	☐ Anger
	☐ Tired

I felt happiest when…

When I'm bored I…

I felt uncomfortable/sad when…

School was…	My parents…
My friends were…	My siblings…

When I think of "someone special" I feel…

I am grateful for…

This was hard but I overcame it by:

This is what I will remember most about today:

MY Crazy TEENAGE LIFE SELF-REFLECTIONS

Date: /   /

When I need support, I can count on…	**Today I Feel:**
My favorite song today is…	☐ Fabulous ☐ In love ☐ Kind of sad ☐ Frustrated
I felt inspired when…	☐ Lonely ☐ Anger ☐ Tired

I felt happiest when…

When I'm bored I…

I felt uncomfortable/sad when…

School was…	My parents…
My friends were…	My siblings…

When I think of "someone special" I feel…

I am grateful for…

This was hard but I overcame it by:

This is what I will remember most about today:

MY Crazy TEENAGE LIFE SELF-REFLECTIONS

Date: /   /

When I need support, I can count on…	**Today I Feel:** ☐ Fabulous ☐ In love ☐ Kind of sad ☐ Frustrated ☐ Lonely ☐ Anger ☐ Tired
My favorite song today is…	
I felt inspired when…	

I felt happiest when…
When I'm bored I…
I felt uncomfortable/sad when…

School was…	My parents…
My friends were…	My siblings…

When I think of "someone special" I feel…
I am grateful for…
This was hard but I overcame it by:
This is what I will remember most about today:

MY Crazy TEENAGE LIFE SELF-REFLECTIONS

Date: /   /

When I need support, I can count on…	**Today I Feel:**
My favorite song today is…	☐ Fabulous ☐ In love ☐ Kind of sad
I felt inspired when…	☐ Frustrated ☐ Lonely ☐ Anger ☐ Tired

I felt happiest when…

When I'm bored I…

I felt uncomfortable/sad when…

School was…	My parents…
My friends were…	My siblings…

When I think of "someone special" I feel…

I am grateful for…

This was hard but I overcame it by:

This is what I will remember most about today:

MY Crazy TEENAGE LIFE SELF-REFLECTIONS

Date: /   /

When I need support, I can count on…	**Today I Feel:**
	☐ Fabulous
My favorite song today is…	☐ In love
	☐ Kind of sad
	☐ Frustrated
I felt inspired when…	☐ Lonely
	☐ Anger
	☐ Tired

I felt happiest when…

When I'm bored I…

I felt uncomfortable/sad when…

School was…	My parents…
My friends were…	My siblings…

When I think of "someone special" I feel…

I am grateful for…

This was hard but I overcame it by:

This is what I will remember most about today:

MY Crazy TEENAGE LIFE SELF-REFLECTIONS

Date: /   /

When I need support, I can count on...	**Today I Feel:**
My favorite song today is...	☐ Fabulous
	☐ In love
I felt inspired when...	☐ Kind of sad
	☐ Frustrated
	☐ Lonely
	☐ Anger
	☐ Tired

I felt happiest when...
When I'm bored I...
I felt uncomfortable/sad when...

School was...	My parents...
My friends were...	My siblings...

When I think of "someone special" I feel...
I am grateful for...
This was hard but I overcame it by:
This is what I will remember most about today:

MY Crazy TEENAGE LIFE SELF-REFLECTIONS

Date: /   /

When I need support, I can count on…	**Today I Feel:** ☐ Fabulous ☐ In love ☐ Kind of sad ☐ Frustrated ☐ Lonely ☐ Anger ☐ Tired
My favorite song today is…	
I felt inspired when…	

I felt happiest when…
When I'm bored I…
I felt uncomfortable/sad when…

School was…	My parents…
My friends were…	My siblings…

When I think of "someone special" I feel…
I am grateful for…
This was hard but I overcame it by:
This is what I will remember most about today:

MY Crazy TEENAGE LIFE SELF-REFLECTIONS

Date: / /

When I need support, I can count on…	**Today I Feel:**
My favorite song today is…	☐ Fabulous ☐ In love ☐ Kind of sad ☐ Frustrated
I felt inspired when…	☐ Lonely ☐ Anger ☐ Tired

I felt happiest when…

When I'm bored I…

I felt uncomfortable/sad when…

School was…	My parents…
My friends were…	My siblings…

When I think of "someone special" I feel…

I am grateful for…

This was hard but I overcame it by:

This is what I will remember most about today:

MY Crazy TEENAGE LIFE SELF-REFLECTIONS

Date: /   /

When I need support, I can count on…	**Today I Feel:**
My favorite song today is…	☐ Fabulous
	☐ In love
	☐ Kind of sad
I felt inspired when…	☐ Frustrated
	☐ Lonely
	☐ Anger
	☐ Tired

I felt happiest when…

When I'm bored I…

I felt uncomfortable/sad when…

School was…	My parents…
My friends were…	My siblings…

When I think of "someone special" I feel…

I am grateful for…

This was hard but I overcame it by:

This is what I will remember most about today:

MY Crazy TEENAGE LIFE SELF-REFLECTIONS

Date: / /

When I need support, I can count on…	**Today I Feel:**
My favorite song today is…	☐ Fabulous
	☐ In love
	☐ Kind of sad
I felt inspired when…	☐ Frustrated
	☐ Lonely
	☐ Anger
	☐ Tired

I felt happiest when…

When I'm bored I…

I felt uncomfortable/sad when…

School was…	My parents…
My friends were…	My siblings…

When I think of "someone special" I feel…

I am grateful for…

This was hard but I overcame it by:

This is what I will remember most about today:

MY Crazy TEENAGE LIFE SELF-REFLECTIONS

Date: / /

When I need support, I can count on…	**Today I Feel:** ☐ Fabulous ☐ In love ☐ Kind of sad ☐ Frustrated ☐ Lonely ☐ Anger ☐ Tired
My favorite song today is…	
I felt inspired when…	

I felt happiest when…
When I'm bored I…
I felt uncomfortable/sad when…

School was…	My parents…
My friends were…	My siblings…

When I think of "someone special" I feel…
I am grateful for…
This was hard but I overcame it by:
This is what I will remember most about today:

MY Crazy TEENAGE LIFE SELF-REFLECTIONS

Date: / /

When I need support, I can count on…	**Today I Feel:**
My favorite song today is…	☐ Fabulous
	☐ In love
	☐ Kind of sad
I felt inspired when…	☐ Frustrated
	☐ Lonely
	☐ Anger
	☐ Tired

I felt happiest when…

When I'm bored I…

I felt uncomfortable/sad when…

School was…	My parents…
My friends were…	My siblings…

When I think of "someone special" I feel…

I am grateful for…

This was hard but I overcame it by:

This is what I will remember most about today:

MY Crazy TEENAGE LIFE SELF-REFLECTIONS

Date: /   /

When I need support, I can count on…	**Today I Feel:**
My favorite song today is…	☐ Fabulous
	☐ In love
I felt inspired when…	☐ Kind of sad
	☐ Frustrated
	☐ Lonely
	☐ Anger
	☐ Tired

I felt happiest when…

When I'm bored I…

I felt uncomfortable/sad when…

School was…	My parents…
My friends were…	My siblings…

When I think of "someone special" I feel…

I am grateful for…

This was hard but I overcame it by:

This is what I will remember most about today:

MY Crazy TEENAGE LIFE SELF-REFLECTIONS

Date: /   /

When I need support, I can count on...	**Today I Feel:**
My favorite song today is...	☐ Fabulous
	☐ In love
	☐ Kind of sad
I felt inspired when...	☐ Frustrated
	☐ Lonely
	☐ Anger
	☐ Tired

I felt happiest when...

When I'm bored I...

I felt uncomfortable/sad when...

School was...	My parents...
My friends were...	My siblings...

When I think of "someone special" I feel...

I am grateful for...

This was hard but I overcame it by:

This is what I will remember most about today:

MY Crazy TEENAGE LIFE SELF-REFLECTIONS

Date: / /

When I need support, I can count on…	**Today I Feel:** ☐ Fabulous ☐ In love ☐ Kind of sad ☐ Frustrated ☐ Lonely ☐ Anger ☐ Tired
My favorite song today is…	
I felt inspired when…	

I felt happiest when…
When I'm bored I…
I felt uncomfortable/sad when…

School was…	My parents…
My friends were…	My siblings…

When I think of "someone special" I feel…
I am grateful for…
This was hard but I overcame it by:
This is what I will remember most about today:

MY Crazy TEENAGE LIFE SELF-REFLECTIONS

Date: /   /

When I need support, I can count on…	**Today I Feel:**
	☐ Fabulous
My favorite song today is…	☐ In love
	☐ Kind of sad
	☐ Frustrated
I felt inspired when…	☐ Lonely
	☐ Anger
	☐ Tired

I felt happiest when…

When I'm bored I…

I felt uncomfortable/sad when…

School was…	My parents…
My friends were…	My siblings…

When I think of "someone special" I feel…

I am grateful for…

This was hard but I overcame it by:

This is what I will remember most about today:

MY Crazy TEENAGE LIFE SELF-REFLECTIONS

Date: / /

When I need support, I can count on…	**Today I Feel:** ☐ Fabulous ☐ In love ☐ Kind of sad ☐ Frustrated ☐ Lonely ☐ Anger ☐ Tired
My favorite song today is…	
I felt inspired when…	

I felt happiest when…
When I'm bored I…
I felt uncomfortable/sad when…

School was…	My parents…
My friends were…	My siblings…

When I think of "someone special" I feel…
I am grateful for…
This was hard but I overcame it by:
This is what I will remember most about today:

MY Crazy TEENAGE LIFE SELF-REFLECTIONS

Date: /   /

When I need support, I can count on…	**Today I Feel:**
My favorite song today is…	☐ Fabulous
	☐ In love
I felt inspired when…	☐ Kind of sad
	☐ Frustrated
	☐ Lonely
	☐ Anger
	☐ Tired

I felt happiest when…
When I'm bored I…
I felt uncomfortable/sad when…

School was…	My parents…
My friends were…	My siblings…

When I think of "someone special" I feel…
I am grateful for…
This was hard but I overcame it by:
This is what I will remember most about today:

MY Crazy TEENAGE LIFE SELF-REFLECTIONS

Date: ___ / ___ / ___

When I need support, I can count on…	**Today I Feel:**
My favorite song today is…	☐ Fabulous ☐ In love ☐ Kind of sad ☐ Frustrated
I felt inspired when…	☐ Lonely ☐ Anger ☐ Tired

I felt happiest when…
When I'm bored I…
I felt uncomfortable/sad when…

School was…	My parents…
My friends were…	My siblings…

When I think of "someone special" I feel…
I am grateful for…
This was hard but I overcame it by:
This is what I will remember most about today:

MY Crazy TEENAGE LIFE SELF-REFLECTIONS

Date: / /

When I need support, I can count on…	**Today I Feel:**
My favorite song today is…	☐ Fabulous ☐ In love ☐ Kind of sad ☐ Frustrated
I felt inspired when…	☐ Lonely ☐ Anger ☐ Tired

I felt happiest when…

When I'm bored I…

I felt uncomfortable/sad when…

School was…	My parents…
My friends were…	My siblings…

When I think of "someone special" I feel…

I am grateful for…

This was hard but I overcame it by:

This is what I will remember most about today:

MY Crazy TEENAGE LIFE SELF-REFLECTIONS

Date: /   /

When I need support, I can count on...	**Today I Feel:**
	☐ Fabulous
My favorite song today is...	☐ In love
	☐ Kind of sad
	☐ Frustrated
I felt inspired when...	☐ Lonely
	☐ Anger
	☐ Tired

I felt happiest when...

When I'm bored I...

I felt uncomfortable/sad when...

School was...	My parents...
My friends were...	My siblings...

When I think of "someone special" I feel...

I am grateful for...

This was hard but I overcame it by:

This is what I will remember most about today:

MY Crazy TEENAGE LIFE SELF-REFLECTIONS

Date: / /

When I need support, I can count on…	**Today I Feel:**
My favorite song today is…	☐ Fabulous ☐ In love ☐ Kind of sad ☐ Frustrated
I felt inspired when…	☐ Lonely ☐ Anger ☐ Tired

I felt happiest when…

When I'm bored I…

I felt uncomfortable/sad when…

School was…	My parents…
My friends were…	My siblings…

When I think of "someone special" I feel…

I am grateful for…

This was hard but I overcame it by:

This is what I will remember most about today:

MY Crazy TEENAGE LIFE SELF-REFLECTIONS

Date: /   /

When I need support, I can count on…	**Today I Feel:**
My favorite song today is…	☐ Fabulous
	☐ In love
I felt inspired when…	☐ Kind of sad
	☐ Frustrated
	☐ Lonely
	☐ Anger
	☐ Tired

I felt happiest when…

When I'm bored I…

I felt uncomfortable/sad when…

School was…	My parents…
My friends were…	My siblings…

When I think of "someone special" I feel…

I am grateful for…

This was hard but I overcame it by:

This is what I will remember most about today:

MY Crazy TEENAGE LIFE SELF-REFLECTIONS

Date: / /

When I need support, I can count on…	**Today I Feel:**
My favorite song today is…	☐ Fabulous ☐ In love ☐ Kind of sad ☐ Frustrated
I felt inspired when…	☐ Lonely ☐ Anger ☐ Tired

I felt happiest when…

When I'm bored I…

I felt uncomfortable/sad when…

School was…	My parents…
My friends were…	My siblings…

When I think of "someone special" I feel…

I am grateful for…

This was hard but I overcame it by:

This is what I will remember most about today:

MY Crazy TEENAGE LIFE SELF-REFLECTIONS

Date: /   /

When I need support, I can count on…	**Today I Feel:**
My favorite song today is…	☐ Fabulous ☐ In love ☐ Kind of sad ☐ Frustrated
I felt inspired when…	☐ Lonely ☐ Anger ☐ Tired

I felt happiest when…
When I'm bored I…
I felt uncomfortable/sad when…

School was…	My parents…
My friends were…	My siblings…

When I think of "someone special" I feel…
I am grateful for…
This was hard but I overcame it by:
This is what I will remember most about today:

MY Crazy TEENAGE LIFE SELF-REFLECTIONS

Date: / /

When I need support, I can count on…	**Today I Feel:**
My favorite song today is…	☐ Fabulous
	☐ In love
I felt inspired when…	☐ Kind of sad
	☐ Frustrated
	☐ Lonely
	☐ Anger
	☐ Tired

I felt happiest when…

When I'm bored I…

I felt uncomfortable/sad when…

School was…	My parents…
My friends were…	My siblings…

When I think of "someone special" I feel…

I am grateful for…

This was hard but I overcame it by:

This is what I will remember most about today:

MY Crazy TEENAGE LIFE SELF-REFLECTIONS

Date: /   /

When I need support, I can count on…	**Today I Feel:** ☐ Fabulous ☐ In love ☐ Kind of sad ☐ Frustrated ☐ Lonely ☐ Anger ☐ Tired
My favorite song today is…	
I felt inspired when…	

I felt happiest when…
When I'm bored I…
I felt uncomfortable/sad when…

School was…	My parents…
My friends were…	My siblings…

When I think of "someone special" I feel…
I am grateful for…
This was hard but I overcame it by:
This is what I will remember most about today:

MY Crazy TEENAGE LIFE SELF-REFLECTIONS

Date: /   /

When I need support, I can count on…	**Today I Feel:**
My favorite song today is…	☐ Fabulous
	☐ In love
I felt inspired when…	☐ Kind of sad
	☐ Frustrated
	☐ Lonely
	☐ Anger
	☐ Tired

I felt happiest when…

When I'm bored I…

I felt uncomfortable/sad when…

School was…	My parents…
My friends were…	My siblings…

When I think of "someone special" I feel…

I am grateful for…

This was hard but I overcame it by:

This is what I will remember most about today:

MY Crazy TEENAGE LIFE SELF-REFLECTIONS

Date: /   /

When I need support, I can count on…	**Today I Feel:**
	☐ Fabulous
My favorite song today is…	☐ In love
	☐ Kind of sad
	☐ Frustrated
I felt inspired when…	☐ Lonely
	☐ Anger
	☐ Tired

I felt happiest when…
When I'm bored I…
I felt uncomfortable/sad when…

School was…	My parents…
My friends were…	My siblings…

When I think of "someone special" I feel…
I am grateful for…
This was hard but I overcame it by:
This is what I will remember most about today:

MY Crazy TEENAGE LIFE SELF-REFLECTIONS

Date: / /

When I need support, I can count on...	**Today I Feel:**
	☐ Fabulous
My favorite song today is...	☐ In love
	☐ Kind of sad
	☐ Frustrated
I felt inspired when...	☐ Lonely
	☐ Anger
	☐ Tired

I felt happiest when...

When I'm bored I...

I felt uncomfortable/sad when...

School was...	My parents...
My friends were...	My siblings...

When I think of "someone special" I feel...

I am grateful for...

This was hard but I overcame it by:

This is what I will remember most about today:

MY Crazy TEENAGE LIFE SELF-REFLECTIONS

Date: /   /

When I need support, I can count on…	**Today I Feel:**
	☐ Fabulous
My favorite song today is…	☐ In love
	☐ Kind of sad
	☐ Frustrated
I felt inspired when…	☐ Lonely
	☐ Anger
	☐ Tired

I felt happiest when…

When I'm bored I…

I felt uncomfortable/sad when…

School was…	My parents…
My friends were…	My siblings…

When I think of "someone special" I feel…

I am grateful for…

This was hard but I overcame it by:

This is what I will remember most about today:

MY Crazy TEENAGE LIFE SELF-REFLECTIONS

Date: /   /

When I need support, I can count on...	**Today I Feel:**
My favorite song today is...	☐ Fabulous
	☐ In love
	☐ Kind of sad
I felt inspired when...	☐ Frustrated
	☐ Lonely
	☐ Anger
	☐ Tired

I felt happiest when...

When I'm bored I...

I felt uncomfortable/sad when...

School was...	My parents...
My friends were...	My siblings...

When I think of "someone special" I feel...

I am grateful for...

This was hard but I overcame it by:

This is what I will remember most about today:

MY Crazy TEENAGE LIFE SELF-REFLECTIONS

Date: /   /

When I need support, I can count on…	**Today I Feel:**
My favorite song today is…	☐ Fabulous ☐ In love ☐ Kind of sad ☐ Frustrated
I felt inspired when…	☐ Lonely ☐ Anger ☐ Tired

I felt happiest when…
When I'm bored I…
I felt uncomfortable/sad when…

School was…	My parents…
My friends were…	My siblings…

When I think of "someone special" I feel…
I am grateful for…
This was hard but I overcame it by:
This is what I will remember most about today:

MY Crazy TEENAGE LIFE SELF-REFLECTIONS

Date: / /

When I need support, I can count on...	**Today I Feel:**
My favorite song today is...	☐ Fabulous
	☐ In love
	☐ Kind of sad
I felt inspired when...	☐ Frustrated
	☐ Lonely
	☐ Anger
	☐ Tired

I felt happiest when...

When I'm bored I...

I felt uncomfortable/sad when...

School was...	My parents...
My friends were...	My siblings...

When I think of "someone special" I feel...

I am grateful for...

This was hard but I overcame it by:

This is what I will remember most about today:

MY Crazy TEENAGE LIFE SELF-REFLECTIONS

Date: / /

When I need support, I can count on…	**Today I Feel:**
	☐ Fabulous
My favorite song today is…	☐ In love
	☐ Kind of sad
	☐ Frustrated
I felt inspired when…	☐ Lonely
	☐ Anger
	☐ Tired

I felt happiest when…
When I'm bored I…
I felt uncomfortable/sad when…

School was…	My parents…
My friends were…	My siblings…

When I think of "someone special" I feel…
I am grateful for…
This was hard but I overcame it by:
This is what I will remember most about today:

MY Crazy TEENAGE LIFE SELF-REFLECTIONS

Date: /   /

When I need support, I can count on...	**Today I Feel:**
My favorite song today is...	☐ Fabulous ☐ In love ☐ Kind of sad ☐ Frustrated
I felt inspired when...	☐ Lonely ☐ Anger ☐ Tired

I felt happiest when...

When I'm bored I...

I felt uncomfortable/sad when...

School was...	My parents...
My friends were...	My siblings...

When I think of "someone special" I feel...

I am grateful for...

This was hard but I overcame it by:

This is what I will remember most about today:

MY Crazy TEENAGE LIFE SELF-REFLECTIONS

Date: /   /

When I need support, I can count on…	**Today I Feel:**
My favorite song today is…	☐ Fabulous
	☐ In love
I felt inspired when…	☐ Kind of sad
	☐ Frustrated
	☐ Lonely
	☐ Anger
	☐ Tired

I felt happiest when…

When I'm bored I…

I felt uncomfortable/sad when…

School was…	My parents…
My friends were…	My siblings…

When I think of "someone special" I feel…

I am grateful for…

This was hard but I overcame it by:

This is what I will remember most about today:

MY Crazy TEENAGE LIFE SELF-REFLECTIONS

Date: / /

When I need support, I can count on...	**Today I Feel:**
My favorite song today is...	☐ Fabulous
	☐ In love
I felt inspired when...	☐ Kind of sad
	☐ Frustrated
	☐ Lonely
	☐ Anger
	☐ Tired

I felt happiest when...
When I'm bored I...
I felt uncomfortable/sad when...

School was...	My parents...
My friends were...	My siblings...

When I think of "someone special" I feel...
I am grateful for...
This was hard but I overcame it by:
This is what I will remember most about today:

My Space
TO WRITE WHATEVER & WHENEVER I WISH

OTHER GUIDED JOURNALS & DIARIES
by
KINYATTA E. GRAY

I Miss You...
Daily Writing Prompts for Reflection, Remembrance, and Spirit Renewal

Fashionista's Travel Diary
A Guided Travel Diary for Travel Planning & Reflections

I'm Doing Me
The Ultimate Breakup Diary for Venting, Reflection & Spirit Renewal

While I'm Still Here
A Guided Expression Journal of Life, Love and Legacy for Those Preparing to Transition

Kinyatta E. Gray is a Best-Selling Author, Travel Influencer and the CEO of FlightsInStilettos, LLC. Kinyatta is also the Chief Beach Towel Designer for the FlightsInStilettos Glam Girl Beach Towels.

Websites:

https://www.flightsinstilettos.com/

https://www.kinyattagray.com/

https://www.honoringmissbee.com/

Disclaimer:
Kinyatta Gray is not a mental health provider and is providing this information based on her personal experiences. If you are experiencing an emotional crisis, seek the help of a professional mental health provider immediately.

www.ingramcontent.com/pod-product-compliance
Lightning Source LLC
Chambersburg PA
CBHW042342300426
44109CB00048B/2674